MY FIRST LOOK

AT PETS

GUINEA PIGS ARE FURRY, FRIENDLY PETS

Guinea Pigs

VALERIE BODDEN

CREATIVE EDUCATION

Published by Creative Education

P.O. Box 227, Mankato, Minnesota 56002

www.thecreativecompany.us

Creative Education is an imprint of The Creative Company

Design by Rita Marshall

Production by CG Book

Photographs by Dreamstime (Ellende, Fordphotouk), Getty Images (Paul Bricknell, C. Dani/I. Jeske, Dorling Kindersley), iStockphoto (Graham Yuile), Oxford (Juniors Bildarchiv)

Copyright © 2009 Creative Education

Printed in the United States of America

Library of Congress Cataloging-in-Publication Data

Bodden, Valerie. Guinea pigs / by Valerie Bodden.

p. cm. — (My first look at pets)

Includes index.

ISBN 978-1-58341-723-2

I. Guinea pigs as pets—Juvenile literature. I. Title. II. Series.

SF459.G9B59 2009   636.935'92—dc22   2007051658

First edition 9 8 7 6 5 4 3 2 1

GUINEA PIGS

SMALL, FURRY PETS

No one knows why guinea pigs are called "pigs." They are not really pigs at all. They are **rodents**.

Guinea pigs are small and furry. Most guinea pigs are about as long as a ruler. They have short legs. They have long teeth that are always growing. They have to chew wood to wear their teeth down.

GUINEA PIGS LIKE TO CHEW ON PIECES OF WOOD

Guinea pigs have small ears. But they can hear very well. Guinea pigs have good senses of sight and smell, too.

Guinea pigs make lots of sounds. They can squeak, squeal, and purr. They can grunt. When they are mad or scared, they chatter their teeth.

Guinea pigs are different
from other rodents because
they do not have tails.

GUINEA PIGS MAY PURR WHEN IT IS TIME TO EAT

Choosing a Guinea Pig

There are many **breeds** of guinea pigs. Some guinea pig breeds have long, smooth hair. Others have short hair. Guinea pigs with short hair can be easier to take care of. They do not need as much **grooming**.

Guinea pigs come in lots of colors. They can be black, white, tan, or brown. Or they can be more than one color.

Some guinea pigs have
hair that is more than
20 inches (50 cm) long!

Most guinea pigs like to live with other guinea pigs. They get lonely when they are by themselves. It is best to keep two female guinea pigs together. Two male guinea pigs might fight. A male and female guinea pig might have babies.

GUINEA PIG CARE

Guinea pigs need to be kept in a cage. The floor of the cage should be covered with bedding such as shredded newspaper or hay. The cage should be cleaned often.

GUINEA PIGS HAVE ABOUT THREE BABIES AT A TIME

Guinea pigs need healthy food. They like to eat hay, special guinea pig food, fruits, and vegetables. Guinea pigs need fresh water, too.

Most guinea pigs should be brushed once a week. Guinea pigs with long hair should be brushed every day. Guinea pigs need baths only if they get dirty.

AN APPLE SLICE IS A GOOD GUINEA PIG SNACK

Just like kids, guinea pigs need regular checkups. A **veterinarian**, or vet, checks guinea pigs to make sure they are healthy. Most pet guinea pigs live four to six years.

Guinea Pig Fun

Guinea pigs are friendly animals. They like to spend lots of time with their owners. Most guinea pigs like to be petted. Some like to be held.

Guinea pigs say

"hello" to each other

by touching noses.

GOOD FOOD HELPS KEEP GUINEA PIGS HEALTHY

Guinea pigs need to be held with two hands. One hand should be around the guinea pig's chest. The other hand should be under its bottom.

Guinea pigs need to spend some time outside their cages every day. They like to run around. Some guinea pigs like to hide in boxes. Others like to play with little balls. Whatever they are doing, all guinea pigs like to know that their owners love them!

A CARDBOARD TUBE CAN BE A FUN GUINEA PIG TOY

Hands-on: Hearing Test

Guinea pigs have a very good sense of hearing. Try this activity with a friend to test your ears.

What You Need

Eight plastic Easter eggs

Dry noodles

Pennies

Water

Dry rice

Stones

Sand

Grass clippings

Paper clips

What You Do

1. Fill each plastic egg with a different item. Do not let your friend see what you put in the eggs.
2. Shake each egg as your friend listens. Let your friend try to guess what is in the eggs.
3. Compare the guesses to what was in each egg. How did your friend do?
4. Now have your friend fill the eggs and test you!

GUINEA PIGS CAN HEAR AND SMELL VERY WELL

Index

Words to Know

breeds—different types of one kind of animal; for example, collies and Labradors are breeds of dogs

grooming—cleaning and brushing

rodents—small, furry animals that chew a lot; mice and hamsters are rodents

veterinarian—an animal doctor

Read More

Coppendale, Jean. *You and Your Pet Guinea Pig.* Irvine, Cal.: QEB, 2004.

Hughes, Sarah. *My Guinea Pig.* New York: Children's Press, 2001.

Ross, Veronica. *My First Guinea Pig.* North Mankato, Minn.: Thameside Press, 2002.

Explore the Web

Guineapigzworld http://www.freewebs.com/guineapigzworld/

Guinea Pigs Club: Games http://www.guineapigsclub.com/gp_site/game.asp

ASPCA Animaland Pet Care: Guinea Pigs

http://www.aspca.org/site/PageServer?pagename=kids_pc_guinea_411